W9-CEM-970

THE TET OFFENSIVE

Graceland Park-O'Donnell Heights
Elementary School #240

THE TET OFFENSIVE

Charles Wills

Silver Burdett Press, Inc.
Englewood Cliffs, New Jersey

Acknowledgments

The author thanks the following individuals and institutions for their invaluable help in text and photo research: Nat Andriani, AP/Wide World Photos; Bill Clark, U.S. Department of the Interior, National Park Service; the Department of Defense Still Media Records Center; Shirley Green; Dr. Douglas Pike, the Indochina Archives, University of California at Berkeley; and Linda M. Cajka, Ken Carter, Arthur S. Hardyman, and Sheila M. S. Hein, the U.S. Army Center of Military History.

Consultants:

We thank the following people for reviewing the manuscript and offering their helpful suggestions:

Michael Kort
Associate Professor of Social Science
Boston University

Richard M. Haynes
Assistant Professor
Division of Administration, Curriculum and Instruction
Director of the Office of Field Experiences and Teacher Placement
School of Education and Psychology
Western Carolina University

Cover, title page, and contents page photos courtesy of the U.S. Army.

Library of Congress Cataloging-in-Publication Data

Wills, Charles.
    The Tet offensive/by Charles Wills.
      p. cm.—(Turning points in American history)
    Bibliography: p.
    Includes index.
    Summary: Describes the massive offensive launched by the Viet Cong during the Tet holiday in 1968 and places it in the context of the entire Vietnamese conflict.
    1. Tet Offensive, 1968—Juvenile literature. [1. Tet Offensive, 1968. 2. Vietnamese Conflict, 1961-1975—Campaigns.] I. Title. II. Series.
DS557.8.T4W55 1989
959.704'84—dc20   89-6186
    ISBN 0-382-09855-2 (pbk.) ISBN 0-382-09849-8   CIP
(lib. bdg.)   AC

Editorial coordination by Richard G. Gallin

 Created by Media Projects Incorporated

C. Carter Smith, *Executive Editor*
Toni Rachiele, *Managing Editor*
Jacqueline Ogburn, *Project Editor*
Bernard Schleifer, *Design Consultant*
Simon Hu, *Cartographer*

Copyright © 1989 by Silver Burdett Press, Inc., a division of Simon & Schuster, Englewood Cliffs, New Jersey.

All rights reserved, including the right of reproduction in whole or in part in any form.

Manufactured in the United States of America.

ISBN 0-382-09849-8   [lib. bdg.]
10 9 8 7 6 5 4 3 2 1

ISBN 0-382-09855-2   [pbk.]
10 9 8 7 6 5 4 3 2 1

CONTENTS

INTRODUCTION

JANUARY 31, 1968

The warm night air was filled with the sounds of celebration in Saigon, capital of South Vietnam, on January 31, 1968. It was the second night of Tet, the holiday marking the Vietnamese new year. The city's population, swelled by visitors from the countryside, was opening the Year of the Monkey with feasting, processions, and fireworks. At 2:00 A.M., twenty men assembled in a garage on a street a few blocks away from the brand-new U.S. embassy compound. These men were not holiday revelers. They were Vietcong—Communist guerrillas dedicated to overthrowing South Vietnam's government and driving the forces of its chief ally, the United States, from the country.

Along with thousands of their comrades, they had slipped into Saigon weeks before, dressed in ordinary clothing, mingling with crowds of Vietnam-

Ellsworth Bunker, U.S. ambassador to South Vietnam, inspects damage to the U.S. embassy in Saigon.

ese traveling to the city for the holiday. Their weapons—explosives, rockets, and automatic rifles—had been smuggled into the city in carts of farm produce, under the eyes of the American and South Vietnamese soldiers. Their leaders had given them a mission from which there was little chance of returning. They were to attack the U.S. embassy. The embassy, completed only a few weeks before at a cost of several million dollars, was Saigon's most prominent symbol of the American commitment to South Vietnam. This commitment had brought over 500,000 U.S. servicemen and -women to Vietnam. Vietcong leaders knew that an attack on the embassy would shake the confidence of Saigon's citizens in their American allies.

At 2:45 A.M. the guerrillas clambered into a truck and a taxi and drove to the embassy. They fired on two guards, who quickly entered the grounds, shutting the embassy gate behind them.

The guerrillas blasted a hole in the embassy wall with plastic explosive and climbed through it. There was a brief exchange of gunfire; two guards and several of the attackers fell dead. The remaining guerrillas raced for the six-story chancery building, the heart of the embassy compound, but the chancery guards managed to shut the building's massive teak doors.

The Americans inside the embassy hastily assembled a force to repel the attackers, who were keeping up a steady stream of automatic rifle and rocket fire in the empty chancery lobby. The embassy's marine guards radioed for reinforcements and held back the Vietcong until help arrived. By morning, all the infiltrators were dead. Five Americans had also been killed.

In the confusion of the attack, American correspondents mistakenly reported that the U.S. embassy had been captured. The American public was stunned. Just four days before, the American commander in Vietnam, General William C. Westmoreland, had sent an optimistic report to Washington. The Vietcong were supposed to be "on the ropes," teetering on the edge of defeat. How had the supposedly weak Vietcong managed to launch an attack on the U.S. embassy in the heart of the South Vietnamese capital?

Three weeks before, on January 8, 1968, the U.S. embassy had released to the American press a document captured from the Vietcong. It contained orders from Vietcong leaders to their field commanders: "Use very strong

military attacks in coordination with the uprisings of the local population to take over towns and cities. . . . Move toward liberating the capital city." But the officers and diplomats at the embassy ignored the document. The possibility of an attack within the city seemed too remote to take seriously, even though the Vietcong still controlled much of the countryside. They had launched attacks in Saigon before, it was true—they had even bombed the old U.S. embassy in March 1965. But that was almost three years ago, before the massive buildup of U.S. troops.

American and South Vietnamese commanders were more concerned with the battles that had broken out on South Vietnam's borders with Laos and North Vietnam, and with the siege of the base Khe Sanh. These battles were fought against troops from Communist North Vietnam. In addition to sending troops to fight in South Vietnam, North Vietnam helped train, supply, and direct the Vietcong guerrillas.

The intelligence officers decided the captured document was just a piece of Vietcong propaganda. After all, the Vietcong had agreed to an eight-day holiday cease-fire. Believing that the Vietcong were sincere, and too weak and disorganized to mount a major offensive, the Army of the Republic of Vietnam (ARVN) had given half its troops leave to spend the holiday with their families.

But there were other signs that a major offensive was being prepared. A few days before, two Vietcong political agents had been captured in Qui Nhon province carrying a tape of revolutionary slogans. It was to be broadcast in Qui Nhon once the radio station had been taken over. South Vietnamese soldiers had captured guerrillas bearing detailed plans for attacks on towns and cities. In the capital of North Vietnam, Hanoi, newspapers openly predicted that a "historic" campaign was about to begin.

One American officer did not ignore these warning signs. Army General Frederick C. Weyand commanded the U.S. troops in and around Saigon. Weyand guessed that the battles along the Vietnamese border were diversions intended to draw American attention from the cities. Intelligence reports of unusual Vietcong activities around Saigon added to his fears. Weyand took his suspicions to General William Westmoreland, and Westmoreland ordered fifteen battalions to take up positions in and around Saigon.

Now, with the rattle of machine gun fire and the thump of explosives replacing the sounds of celebration in Saigon's streets, Weyand's suspicions were confirmed. The attack on the embassy was only a small part of the battle now raging in and around Saigon. The Vietcong, supported by the North Vietnamese Army (NVA), were launching attacks throughout the rest of South

General William C. Westmoreland, American commander in Vietnam from 1964 to 1968, arrives at the U.S. embassy in Saigon the morning after the Vietcong attack.

Vietnam as well. By the next day, 105 South Vietnamese towns and cities and scores of American and Vietnamese military installations, from the Demilitarized Zone in the north to the Mekong River Delta in the south, were under attack. Not since the Battle of the Bulge in World War II had American forces received such a shock.

1

THE COMMITMENT BEGINS

Vietnam, a nation slightly larger than the state of Arizona, is a narrow strip of land on the Southeast Asian peninsula south of China. It is bordered to the east by the South China Sea and the Gulf of Tonkin and to the west by the Gulf of Thailand and by Laos and Cambodia, two small nations whose histories have always been linked with Vietnam's. The country is bordered on the north by China. Two great rivers and their deltas—the Red River in the north and the Mekong River in the south—dominate the land. Between these river deltas lies a landscape of deep jungle, rugged mountain ranges, and forested plateaus.

For much of its early history Vietnam was dominated by its powerful neighbor, China. But the Vietnamese people cherished their independence and they

Saigon, seen here in the 1950s, was once known as the "Paris of the Orient."

fought hard for it, even though they absorbed much of China's culture. By the fifteenth century the Chinese had been driven from Vietnam.

Portuguese sailors arrived in Vietnam in 1535, and they were followed by Dutch, French, and English traders over the next three centuries. France gradually emerged as the colonial power in Indochina. In the early nineteenth century, French soldiers landed in Vietnam. They originally came to protect the French missionaries, but over the next half century, in spite of resistance against their domination, France had added Vietnam, Laos, and Cambodia to its colonial empire, completing its control of Indochina by 1887. The region was organized into the Indochinese Union, consisting of the states of Tonkin in the north, Annam in the central part of Vietnam, and Cochin China (including Cambodia) in the south. Six years later Laos was added to the Union.

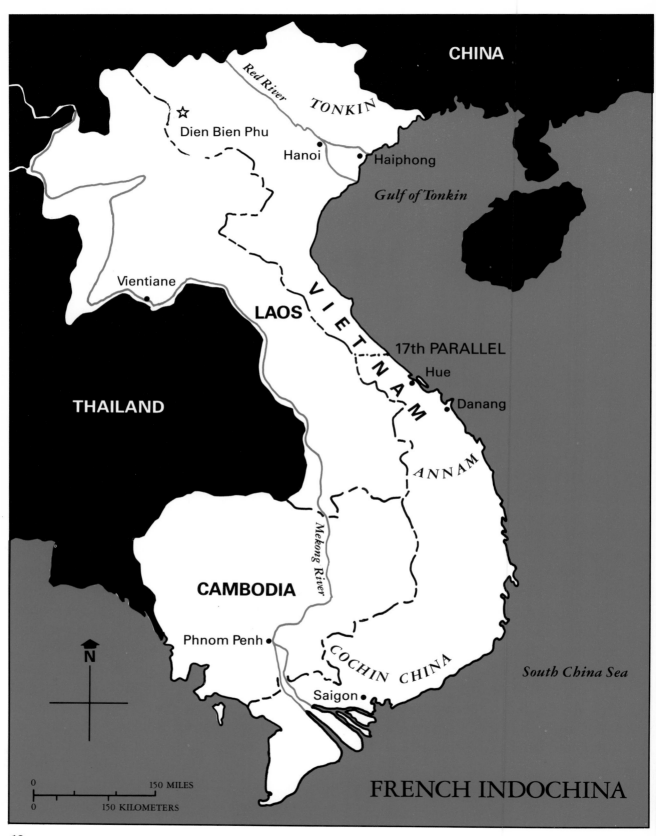

CHINA

TONKIN

Red River

☆
Dien Bien Phu

Hanoi • • Haiphong

Gulf of Tonkin

VIETNAM

Vientiane •

LAOS

17th PARALLEL

• Hue

THAILAND

Danang •

ANNAM

Mekong River

CAMBODIA

Phnom Penh •

N

COCHIN CHINA

Saigon •

South China Sea

0		150 MILES
0		150 KILOMETERS

FRENCH INDOCHINA

France ran Indochina as a very profitable colony for over fifty years. The native population, consisting mostly of landless peasants raising rice for subsistence, continued to oppose French domination, but there was little they could do in the face of French power.

This situation changed when Japanese troops occupied Indochina during World War II. The Japanese occupation gave the Vietnamese nationalists the opportunity they had long awaited. In May 1941, Ho Chi Minh, a prominent nationalist and a Moscow-trained Communist agent, formed the League for the Independence of Vietnam, called the Vietminh. The Vietminh, based in southern China, hoped to win independence for Vietnam by liberating it from the Japanese. By 1945 Vietminh units inside Vietnam were conducting guerrilla operations. They were aided by the American OSS (the Office of Strategic Services, a forerunner of the Central Intelligence Agency), which provided the Vietminh with weapons and advisers in a return for Vietminh aid to American pilots shot down in the China-Vietnam border area. On September 2, 1945, the same day Japan surrendered, Ho Chi Minh proclaimed an independent Democratic Republic of Vietnam in the Tonkinese capital of Hanoi.

But the situation in Indochina was too confused to allow an easy transition to independence. As the Japanese occupation ended, British troops moved into southern Vietnam and Nationalist

Ho Chi Minh at a 1946 conference in France. For a short time it seemed as if Vietnam would gain its independence peacefully.

NATIONAL ARCHIVES

Chinese forces entered the north to keep order. The Chinese soon withdrew, but the British let French forces reain control of Laos, Cambodia, and Vietnam up to the 16th parallel of latitude. The French, at first appearing to recognize Ho's government, within a year decided to restore their prewar colonial empire. They chose at first to negotiate, and offered Vietnam limited independence as part of the Indochinese Federation of the French Union, a creation they hoped would function as the British Commonwealth did. They proposed Bao Dai, a member of the Vietnamese nobility, as Vietnam's leader. Some Vietnamese accepted this, but Ho Chi Minh and his followers did not.

Negotiations broke down. In March 1946, fighting broke out in Hanoi. French troops drove Ho and the Vietminh from the city into the jungles of northeast Vietnam, and the conflict between the French and the Vietminh, the First Indochina War, had begun.

It was to last for nine bitter years. In the early years of the war, the Vietminh hid in the countryside, while the French constructed a network of fortifications around Hanoi and the populous Red River Delta. Fighting was infrequent. That was just what Ho wanted, for it gave him time to make his ill-equipped Vietminh into an efficient fighting force. He turned over leadership of the military part of the Vietminh to Vo Nguyen Giap, a former history teacher. Giap was a student of the guerrilla warfare techniques developed by the Chinese Communist leader Mao Zedong (Mao

Tse-tung). Giap avoided fixed battles, in which the superior firepower of the French forces would overpower the lightly armed Vietminh. Instead, Giap concentrated on ambushing French patrols and sabotaging supply lines to weaken French morale and tie down French troops. By the early 1950s the war was a stalemate. French commanders believed the only way to defeat the Vietminh was to lure them into the open.

The French prepared for a major confrontation. Dien Bien Phu was a valley near the Laotian border, about 170 miles from Hanoi. The plan was to establish a large base on the valley floor which could be easily resupplied by air. The French planned to cut the supply lines from Laos to the Vietminh. If the Vietminh attacked Dien Bien Phu, the French believed, they would be destroyed by the base's superior firepower like waves breaking on a rock. On November 20, 1953, French paratroops dropped on Dien Bien Phu, and within a few weeks about 10,000 soldiers were in position.

But the French had underestimated the Vietminh's strength. Giap's soldiers, dug into camouflaged and protected positions in the surrounding mountains, outnumbered the French by more than four to one. For every Vietminh soldier there was a porter on a network of narrow mountain trails, bringing ammunition and supplies from Vietminh sanctuaries in Laos on a converted bicycle or on his back. Also, Giap's force—which was now receiving weapons from the

INDOCHINA ARCHIVES, BERKELEY

May 7, 1954: Victorious Vietminh soldiers raise their flag over the French command bunker at Dien Bien Phu, bringing the 55-day siege—and French rule in Vietnam—to an end.

Soviet Union and Communist China—was better armed than the French. On March 13, the Vietminh artillery began raining shells on the French garrison.

The siege lasted 55 days. One by one the French outposts surrounding Dien Bien Phu fell. On May 7, 1954, the base surrendered and the dispirited, defeated French troops were marched into captivity. Opposition to the war had become widespread in France, and the French government decided to seek a cease-fire.

As the Vietminh were making their final assault on Dien Bien Phu, representatives from France, Great Britain, the United States, China, and the Soviet Union met in conference in Geneva, Switzerland, to discuss the future of Indochina. The representatives agreed that all French forces were to be with-drawn from Indochina. Laos and Cambodia were to become independent states, and Vietnam was to be temporarily partitioned along the 17th parallel of latitude. The land to the north of that line became known as the Democratic Republic of Vietnam, with a Communist government headed by Ho Chi Minh. South Vietnam was now called The Republic of Vietnam, led by Bao Dai. In 1956, the United Nations was to sponsor an election in which the people of both North and South Vietnam would participate. The election would decide what form of government the two nations would have when united. On July 21, 1954, the Geneva Accords were signed.

Following World War II the United States adopted a hands-off policy toward Indochina. While many in Washington distrusted Ho's close ties with Moscow, the State Department did not want the United States associated with France's attempt to reestablish its colonial empire. The struggle between the Vietminh and the French was considered, in the words of an American military historian, "a distant backwater struggle." That view changed when tensions between the United States and the Soviet Union heightened into the cold war. In 1947, President Truman proclaimed the "Truman Doctrine," a policy of American aid for nations struggling with Communist rebels. American foreign policy became dominated by the idea of containment—that Communist expansion had to be halted and contained by the West.

Two events in particular shaped the new U.S. attitude toward Indochina. The victory of Mao Zedong over the American-supported Nationalists in China convinced many that communism would dominate Asia unless it was stopped. In the Korean War of 1950–1953, American and United Nations forces had prevented Communist North Korea from conquering South Korea. This made some military planners confident that a "limited" land war in Asia could be won. Since the Vietminh were now considered part of the Communist threat in Asia, the American position toward Indochina grew into one of support for the French.

Direct American aid to the French had actually begun as early as May 1950. Over the next four years American aid increased until the United States

Ngo Dinh Diem, president of South Vietnam, is welcomed by President Dwight Eisenhower and Secretary of State John Foster Dulles during a 1957 visit to the United States.

was providing almost 80 percent of the cost of the French war effort. The United States supplied everything from uniforms to airplanes to the French. Although no American troops were sent to Vietnam, some of President Dwight Eisenhower's military advisers pressed him to help the French during the siege of Dien Bien Phu—to order air strikes from U.S. carriers against Vietminh positions or even to drop atomic bombs around the base. Eisenhower rejected these suggestions. The war in Korea had ended less than a year earlier, and the American public would not be likely

INDOCHINA ARCHIVES, BERKELEY

to support another war in Asia—at least for the moment.

Within a year of the fall of Dien Bien Phu, leadership of South Vietnam passed from Bao Dai to the man who had served as his premier, Ngo Dinh Diem, a Vietnamese aristocrat, a Roman Catholic, and a former civil servant for the French colonial government. He had left Vietnam in 1933 after an argument with the French. Ho Chi Minh, aware of Diem's nationalist views, sought his support after World War II, but Diem refused to cooperate with Ho. Diem returned to Vietnam in 1954, and now faced the task of leading the new and struggling nation.

Diem faced tremendous problems. After the Vietminh marched into Hanoi, some 860,000 refugees had fled from North Vietnam to South Vietnam, placing a strain on South Vietnam's underdeveloped economy. Many of these refugees were Catholics fearing religious persecution under the new Communist government. The Vietnamese Buddhists, on the other hand, mistrusted Diem's Catholicism and protested his policy of giving land grants to Catholic refugees from the north while many southern peasants had little or no land. Bloody fighting broke out in Saigon between government forces and the private armies of several religious and political sects. Roads, communications, and industry were in a state of near chaos. Without aid and assistance, South Vietnam would fall. Diem found that aid and assistance in the United States.

A Vietcong unit poses in a jungle camp. The guerrillas sitting at the left of the photo hold field radios captured from South Vietnamese troops.

CENTER OF MILITARY HISTORY

HEARTS AND MINDS

U.S. MARINE CORPS PHOTO

Between 1955 and 1960 over $2 billion in American aid flowed into South Vietnam. Three-quarters of the aid was military, for the United States wanted a strong, independent South Vietnam as a defense against further Communist expansion in Southeast Asia. An American Military Advisory Group (MAG) began reorganizing, training, and equipping the South Vietnamese army. Civilian advisers and technicians arrived to assist with agriculture, transportation, manufacturing, and education.

But Diem's control of South Vietnam was precarious, despite American support. When he refused to honor the 1954 Geneva Accords and the election they mandated for 1956—because he believed many voters would call for unification with North Vietnam—he alienated many South Vietnamese. The or-

American marines on patrol pass peasants in the South Vietnamese countryside.

dinary citizen also saw that most of the political power in the South was wielded by Diem's close friends and family and wondered how much he would benefit from the Diem government. Diem's stormy eight-year reign was marked by attempted coups and assassinations, violent demonstrations, and internal corruption.

While Diem struggled to maintain power in Saigon, the situation in the countryside worsened. Most government attempts at land reform failed. Diem angered villagers by replacing village leaders with bureaucratic appointees with little understanding of local needs. In ignoring the Vietnamese tradition that "the authority of the government ends at the village gate," Diem lost the support of much of the peasant population. Dissatisfaction with Diem and his government in the countryside was widespread by 1957.

In that year guerrillas, many of them former Vietminh, began to operate against government outposts in the Me-

U.S. ARMY PHOTO

Lt. Colonel John Paul Vann (left) of the U.S. army confers with American and South Vietnamese officers in 1962. Vann spent eight years in Vietnam as both a military and civil adviser.

kong River Delta. The insurgency soon spread to the rest of the country. These guerrillas were organized as the National Liberation Front (NLF) in 1959. They would become better known as the Vietcong—Vietnamese Communists. In some villages this resistance to Saigon had plenty of local support. In others, the Vietcong forced peasants, through violence and terror, into providing recruits, rice, and money for the revolutionary cause.

Ho Chi Minh, still hoping to unite Vietnam under Communist rule, used the growing unrest to his advantage. In May 1959, the North Vietnamese government called for "a strong North Viet-namese base for helping the South Vietnamese to overthrow Diem and expel the United States." Work began on what would become known as the Ho Chi Minh trail—a network of narrow roads snaking through the jungles of Laos and Cambodia. Arms and reinforcements for the "liberation struggle" in the South would soon flow down the trail from North Vietnam. Throughout 1959, the Vietcong grew in strength and their attacks increased. In July, two American Army advisers were killed in a Vietcong attack on Bien Hoa, near Saigon—the first American casualties of this new Indochina war.

South Vietnam's army proved ineffective at fighting the guerrilla war waged by the Vietcong. The Saigon government adopted a strategy of "pacification"—which usually meant relocating peasants from their native villages to fortified compounds in government-controlled areas. This policy further alienated the peasants from the Diem regime. By 1960, some observers estimated that the Vietcong controlled over half of South Vietnam.

In the United States, 1960 was an election year. A new president, the youthful John F. Kennedy, took office, pledging to "pay any price, bear any burden . . . to assure the survival and the success of liberty." He and his advisers—Secretary of Defense Robert McNamara, National Security Adviser Walt Rostow, and military adviser General Maxwell Taylor—were determined to continue the U.S. support for South Vietnam.

In October 1961, Kennedy sent General Taylor to Vietnam on a fact-finding mission. Taylor reported that despite the crisis, Diem was worthy of continued U.S. support. He proposed sending a U.S. combat force to Vietnam to reinforce the ARVN. But President Kennedy decided against sending troops to fight. Instead, the amount of military aid was increased and the number of military advisers was raised to 18,000.

In the early 1960s the United States adopted a strategy of "counterinsurgency" in Vietnam. The goal of counterinsurgency was to undermine support for the Vietcong by winning the "hearts and minds" of the people. Civil pro-

grams—medical care, education, and agricultural aid—were begun. Villagers were armed and trained to defend their homes against the Vietcong. The U.S. Army sent teams of Special Forces soldiers to Vietnam. These highly trained "Green Berets" advised, and sometimes fought alongside, South Vietnamese forces to deny the countryside to the Vietcong. At the same time, American advisers tried to raise the fighting skill and spirit of the regular ARVN forces. Helicopters were sent to Vietnam to increase ARVN mobility.

Despite these measures, the situation in South Vietnam continued to deteriorate. In 1962, Buddhist monks in Saigon launched widespread protests against Diem. Several burned themselves to death in acts of protest that shocked the world. In the countryside, the Vietcong conducted a terror campaign, killing government officials and village leaders who supported Diem. This further weakened the Saigon government. In late 1963, Washington received word that an anti-Diem rebellion was being planned. No move was made to stop it. On November 1, 1963, rebels from the ARVN took control of Saigon and killed Diem.

A few weeks later President Kennedy, too, was felled by an assassin's bullet. The presidency passed to Lyndon Johnson. In the election year of 1964, he assured the public that the United States would not become involved in a "shooting war" in Vietnam. "We are not about to send American boys nine or ten thousand miles to do

THE LYNDON B. JOHNSON LIBRARY

what Asian boys should be doing for themselves," he stated. Still, the number of U.S. advisers was increased to 23,000 in 1964.

On August 2, 1964, the U.S. destroyer *Maddox*, on maneuvers in the Gulf of Tonkin off the coast of North Vietnam, reported an attack by a North Vietnamese torpedo boat. Three days later, another destroyer reported a similar attack. President Johnson retaliated by ordering an American air strike against North Vietnamese naval bases. Congress supported Johnson's action by passing the Gulf of Tonkin Resolution, which gave the president nearly unlimited authority "to take all necessary steps, including the use of armed force" to protect South Vietnam. The resolution was passed almost unanimously, although one senator called it "a predated declaration of war." With the Gulf of Tonkin Resolution, the stage for an American war in Vietnam was set.

American intervention now escalated rapidly. On February 7, 1965, the U.S. compound at Pleiku was attacked by the Vietcong. Eight Americans were killed and more than a hundred wounded. President Johnson immediately ordered retaliatory air raids on North Vietnam. On March 2, the United States began the massive Rolling Thunder bombing offensive against the

Surrounded by members of Congress, President Lyndon Johnson signs the Gulf of Tonkin Resolution on August 10, 1964. Only two senators opposed the measure.

North. It was to last, on and off, for over three years.

On March 8, 1965, two battalions of U.S. Marines landed on a beach near Danang. Their mission was not, at first, to seek out and fight the Vietcong, but to guard the nearby American airbase. U.S. combat troops were now on the ground in South Vietnam, and U.S. aircraft were flying combat missions into North Vietnam.

President Johnson was faced with the decision, in his words, to "run in or run out" of Vietnam—whether or not to send more troops and allow them to engage in combat. On April 2, Johnson made his choice—to run in. He sent more soldiers and Marines to Vietnam. He also ordered the bombing of North Vietnam increased, and he appealed to "allied" nations to send troops and aid to Vietnam. Within two years, 60,000 allied troops, mainly from South Korea and Australia, were fighting alongside the Americans and South Vietnamese, and by the summer of 1965, American soldiers and marines were in combat with the Vietcong and NVA. Although Congress never officially declared war on North Vietnam, 184,000 American troops were in South Vietnam by the end of the year.

American commanders in Vietnam now had to decide how to conduct the war. Some favored an "enclave" strategy. According to this plan, troops would spread out slowly from coastal bases, denying territory to the Vietcong through constant patrolling. But Gen-

U.S. Marines land on Red Beach One near Danang on March 8, 1965.

U.S. MARINE CORPS PHOTO

eral William C. Westmoreland, Commander of all U.S. forces in Vietnam since 1964, favored a more active strategy. He wanted to destroy the communist forces by direct attacks on "main force" NVA and Vietcong units. This would be accomplished by the superior firepower and helicopter-borne mobility of the American forces.

In November 1965, Westmoreland's strategy was put to the test in the Ia Drang Valley when U.S. troops defeated tough, well-armed NVA regulars. Encouraged by this victory, Westmoreland began a series of similar "search and destroy" operations, designed to destroy NVA troops faster than replacements could be moved down the Ho Chi Minh trail. This led to a war of attrition in Vietnam, with U.S. forces attempting to exhaust the NVA and the Vietcong and to break their will to fight. The ultimate goal was not to conquer North Vietnam. That would have required a force of a million or more men, which the American public would not have supported. The measure of victory in Vietnam was not territory captured—the traditional way of winning wars—but the number of enemy killed. Americans became familiar with the phrase "body count"— the number of enemy dead left after an operation. To many in the United States, it seemed a poor way to fight a war, especially a guerrilla war.

In the lowlands and the Mekong River Delta, American and South Vietnamese soldiers faced a determined guerrilla opponent who knew the land and often had the support of the local peasants. The Vietcong were often dressed in ordinary peasant clothes and difficult to distinguish from civilians. American patrols would pass through a seemingly peaceful village, only to be sniped at or mortared a short time later. U.S. forces burned or bombed many villages suspected of sheltering Vietcong. The Vietcong avoided direct battle with the better-armed and more numerous American troops, preferring ambushes. In some parts of the country, particularly the heavily forested "Iron Triangle" near Saigon, the Vietcong operated from elaborate, well-camouflaged tunnel complexes into which they could disappear after attacks.

An American historian described some of the dangers faced by American troops in the countryside:

> On patrol, American troops encountered booby traps set along the trails, in chicken coops and fishing nets. . . . Mines—pressure, trip, or electrically detonated—were everywhere. Trails were sown with sharpened bamboo spikes—punji sticks—which inflicted painful wounds, elephant traps were dug with the bottoms lined with spikes and the fields were planted with long sharpened poles designed to ward off helicopters.

Eventually, U.S. troops built hundreds of "firebases" throughout South Vietnam, to provide artillery support for patrolling infantry. American officers were more likely to call on this artillery, or on air support, than to send

IMAGES OF WAR

Helicopters land 1st Cavalry soldiers on a search-and-destroy mission in 1966.

In a village in Qui Nhon province, soldiers of the 1st Cavalry search a peasant hut for signs of the Vietcong.

U.S. ARMY PHOTO

U.S. ARMY PHOTO

A hut suspected of sheltering local Vietcong guerrillas is burned by American soldiers.

Captured Vietcong guerrillas are taken in for questioning by intelligence specialists.

U.S. ARMY PHOTO

their men into dangerous situations without it. This reliance on firepower over manpower saved American lives, but at the cost of many civilian casualties. Large tracts of South Vietnam were cleared of civilians and designated as "free fire zones." Anyone left was assumed to be the enemy. This strategy, like the relocation of peasants from their villages, made both U.S. and ARVN forces unpopular with many Vietnamese civilians.

For every American combat soldier or marine, there were between six and ten men and women in the rear areas, working to support and supply the troops in the field. Huge U.S. bases were built, mainly near the cities along the coast. The U.S. presence made these areas fairly secure from attack. But in a war without a real front line, no American in Vietnam was truly safe. The Vietcong became skilled at penetrating barbed wire and mine fields to attack American bases. Vietcong agents mingled with civilians to gain intelligence or conduct terror attacks.

American warplanes, sleek Navy fighter-bombers from offshore carriers or huge Air Force B–52 bombers, constantly roared north above the heads of the ground troops. By 1967, 13,000 sorties (one flight by one plane) were being flown each month. The bombing of North Vietnam was intended to force Hanoi into negotiating an end to the war. This did not work. More bombs were dropped on North Vietnam than had been dropped on Germany during all of World War II, but the war went on

and North Vietnam continued to function. From 1965 to 1968, President Johnson periodically ordered halts in the bombing to prove American willingness to negotiate, but the North Vietnamese refused all offers. Some blamed their continued refusal on the restrictions placed on the bombing. American aircrews were ordered to avoid bombing populated places, and many of the most important targets in the North—like Haiphong Harbor, into which Soviet and Chinese supplies flowed—were declared off-limits.

The North Vietnamese also became skilled at defending themselves from air attack. Antiaircraft artillery and missiles shot down many U.S. aircraft. Most of the American prisoners of war taken by North Vietnam were downed American airmen. Some remained in captivity, in terrible conditions, for more than eight years.

As the fighting in Vietnam escalated, a war of words was fought in the United States. By 1967, many Americans had become opposed to the war. Some felt the United States had no right to intervene so forcefully in another country's affairs. Others believed it was hypocritical to fight against communism while supporting the corrupt, repressive military regime in Saigon. The Johnson administration tried to convince the American public that its aim in Vietnam was noble: to help a struggling nation resist North Vietnam's aggression and Vietcong terror. But the images that flashed across American television screens each night were anything but noble. The sight of American soldiers burning huts and devastating the countryside with bombs and napalm enraged many people in the United States and around the world.

Demonstrations against the war began in 1964, even before combat troops had been sent to Vietnam. As the war escalated, antiwar demonstrations increased and the numbers of protesters grew. In April 1967, 125,000 protesters marched in New York City. Four months later, 75,000 protesters attempted to block the entrance to the Pentagon in Washington, D.C. Colleges held "teach-ins" to debate and discuss the war. Young men publicly burned their draft cards, symbols of a conscription system that sent many of them into the military, and perhaps to Vietnam, despite their opposition to the war. Tens of thousands fled to Canada or Europe to avoid the draft.

Many prominent Americans, including civil rights leader Martin Luther King, Jr., added their voices to the growing chorus of protest against the war. Congress, like the American public, split into "hawks" (those who supported the war) and "doves" (those who wanted U.S. forces withdrawn). Dissent reached into Johnson's cabinet. Secretary of Defense Robert McNamara resigned his post in late 1967 after reading the results of a secret study of the war. That study, made public as the "Pentagon Papers" four years later, indicated that the United States was no longer in

U.S. AIR FORCE PHOTO

In a helicopter near the Demilitarized Zone, a crewman prepares to drop a camouflaged sensor, designed to detect the movement of enemy troops or vehicles.

Vietnam to fight Communist aggression but to protect its reputation.

In 1961, President Kennedy had asked French President Charles de Gaulle for advice on Indochina. If you send troops, De Gaulle said, "I predict . . . that you will, step by step, be sucked into a bottomless military and political quagmire." As 1967 drew to a close, President De Gaulle's prediction had turned into reality in the minds of many Americans.

3

"FORWARD! TOTAL VICTORY WILL BE OURS!"

Despite the protests at home and the difficulties of waging war in Vietnam, there were some hopeful signs in the last months of 1967. In the fall, elections were held in South Vietnam, and Nguyen Van Thieu was elected president. The elections brought some stability to the Saigon government.

While the Vietcong remained strong in much of the countryside, the "fire brigade" part of the war was ending. When the United States had entered the war in strength in 1965, the Vietcong and the North Vietnamese Army (NVA) controlled about 80 percent of South Vietnam. Now, much of the country, especially the major cities, was considered secure. If South Vietnam's government could pass into responsible civilian hands, and if its army could be made strong enough to deal with the Communist threat, an American withdrawal

Residents of Cholon, a suburb of Saigon, look for possessions in the wreckage of their homes after the Tet fighting in Saigon.

might come soon. American commanders and politicians proclaimed that the "light at the end of the tunnel" was now visible.

In fact, the American involvement had only thrown off the North Vietnamese and Vietcong timetable. In 1965, Ho Chi Minh and his advisers believed that the years of guerrilla warfare in South Vietnam would soon give way to a national uprising against the Saigon government and its ally, the United States. The arrival of American ground troops had made that impossible. Like President Lyndon Johnson in 1965, Ho now had to decide whether to "run in or run out" of the South. In this case, "running out" would mean reducing the war effort in South Vietnam, giving the Vietcong and NVA time to rebuild their strength. Many of Ho's advisers felt this was the right choice. But Ho believed that time, usually the guerrilla's ally, was now on the American and South Vietnamese side.

INDOCHINA ARCHIVES, BERKELEY

Vo Nguyen Giap. As military commander of the Vietminh, he conducted the siege of Dien Bien Phu in 1954; as North Vietnam's minister of defense, he planned the Tet Offensive.

There were personal considerations for Ho, too. He was about 77 and in poor health. His life had been spent struggling for a united and independent Vietnam, and he did not want to die with this goal unfulfilled. Ho and Vo Nguyen Giap, the victor of Dien Bien Phu, worked out a bold plan. They decided to launch a general offensive against all of South Vietnam: the Vietcong, with the support of the NVA, would attack everywhere at once. There would not be enough American troops to counter such a blow. The South Vietnamese forces, they believed, would fall apart.

The goals for the offensive were political and psychological as well as military. The Vietcong were to attack government offices, police stations, and military headquarters. They were to seize radio stations and broadcast propaganda messages and offers of amnesty to South Vietnamese troops who joined their ranks. By destroying the symbols of the South Vietnamese government, Ho and Giap hoped to spark the long-awaited general uprising.

The date for the offensive was Tet, the Vietnamese people's most sacred holiday. The movement of people just before Tet would hide the movement of NVA troops and Vietcong to their positions in and around the cities. Tet was also traditionally a time for a brief truce. Ho and Giap knew that the South Vietnamese military would be relaxed and unprepared during Tet.

In order for the attacks to succeed, Giap needed the element of surprise. The Vietcong and NVA had to draw American attention and troops from the major towns and cities of the South, so in the fall of 1967 the NVA launched attacks along South Vietnam's borders and the Demilitarized Zone. Battles erupted at U.S. outposts at Con Thien, Dak To, and Khe Sanh.

Khe Sanh was a remote, mountain-ringed base near the Laotian border. On January 21, 1968, Khe Sanh, manned by

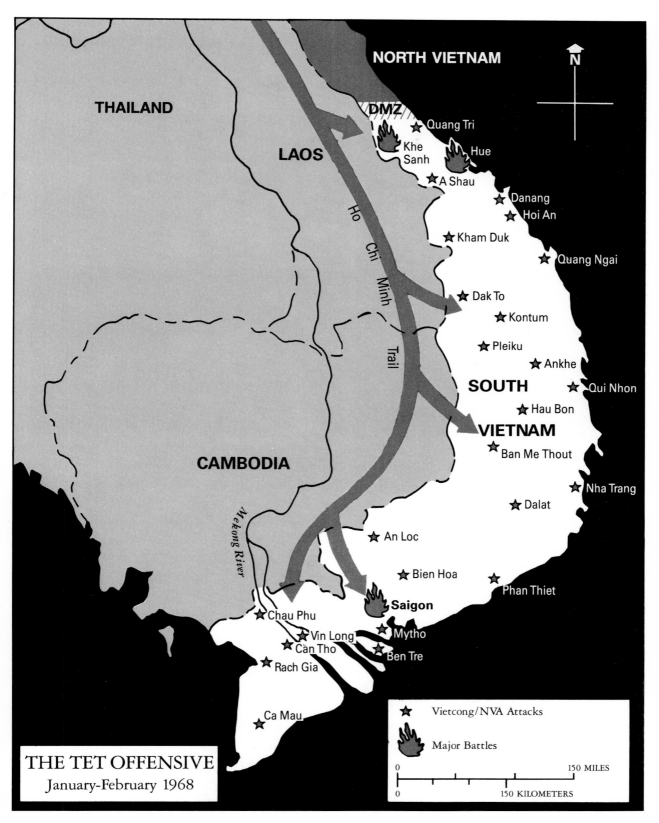

NORTH VIETNAM

THAILAND

LAOS

DMZ

★ Quang Tri

Khe Sanh

Hue

★ A Shau

★ Danang

★ Hoi An

★ Kham Duk

★ Quang Ngai

Ho Chi Minh

Trail

★ Dak To

★ Kontum

★ Pleiku

★ Ankhe

SOUTH

★ Qui Nhon

★ Hau Bon

VIETNAM

★ Ban Me Thout

CAMBODIA

★ Nha Trang

★ Dalat

Mekong River

★ An Loc

★ Bien Hoa

★ Phan Thiet

Saigon

★ Chau Phu

★ Mytho

★ Vin Long

★ Can Tho

★ Ben Tre

★ Rach Gia

★ Ca Mau

★ Vietcong/NVA Attacks

Major Battles

0   150 MILES

0   150 KILOMETERS

THE TET OFFENSIVE
January–February 1968

A North Vietnamese artillery shell crashes into Khe Sanh.

5,000 American marines and 800 South Vietnamese rangers, came under fire from NVA artillery. The base had been surrounded by 20,000 NVA soldiers. Khe Sanh was under siege. Inside the barbed wire the mood grew tense. One American said, "Being in Khe Sanh is like sitting in an electric chair and waiting for someone to pull the switch." On the night of February 7, radio operators at Khe Sanh heard a terrifying report from Lang Vei, an Army Special Forces camp just below Khe Sanh: "There are tanks in our wire!" A large NVA force, aided by Soviet-supplied tanks, overran the camp. It was the first time American troops in Vietnam had faced an armored enemy.

In Saigon and Washington, Khe Sanh raised the ghost of Dien Bien Phu. There were rumors that Giap himself was directing the siege, as he had done at Dien Bien Phu. Actually, Giap was ill and in Hanoi.

At first, the situation at Khe Sanh did seem like that at Dien Bien Phu 24 years before. The marines at Khe Sanh were greatly outnumbered, as the French had been. Both bases were in rugged country—the only way in or out was by air. President Johnson took a keen interest in Khe Sanh. He realized that a defeat there would reduce public support for an already unpopular conflict. He had a model of the base at Khe Sanh built in the White House basement so he could personally follow the progress of the siege.

But there were differences between Khe Sanh and Dien Bien Phu. Unlike the French, the Americans had more artillery than did the NVA. The marines could count on steady delivery of supplies by cargo planes and helicopters. Most important, they could call on air support, especially from B–52 bombers. Despite NVA infantry, artillery, and rocket attacks, the defenders held on.

Giap never wanted Khe Sanh to be a second Dien Bien Phu. Like the border battles, it was meant to draw American attention from the Vietcong and NVA

This view of Khe Sanh shows the network of bunkers and trenches constructed by the American marines and South Vietnamese rangers, as well as the wreckage of an aircraft destroyed by mortar fire.

U.S. MARINE CORPS PHOTO

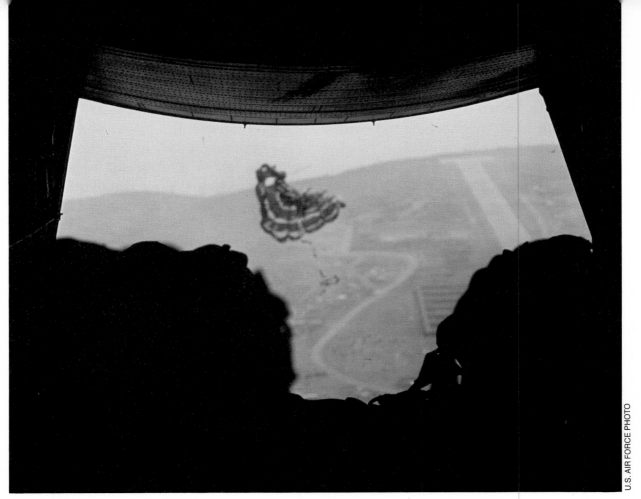

A C-130 transport parachutes a load of supplies to the besieged marines at Khe Sanh.

U.S. AIR FORCE PHOTO

buildup farther south. General Westmoreland reinforced I-Corps, the northernmost battle zone in South Vietnam. He believed North Vietnam might be about to launch an invasion across the DMZ.

While the NVA besieged Khe Sanh, Vietcong units throughout South Vietnam prepared for the coming offensive. Soldiers trained with new weapons from North Vietnam. The political cadres made lists of Vietnamese who had cooperated with the Saigon government and U.S. forces. They were to be punished when the Vietcong gained control of the towns and cities. Vietcong and NVA units gathered silently around the offensive's targets—thirty-six provincial capitals, sixty-four district capitals, five major cities, and scores of American and South Vietnamese military bases. Vietcong guerrillas put on civilian clothing, or even South Vietnamese uniforms, and slipped into the cities among the holiday crowds. As the end of January approached, 70,000 NVA

January 31, 1968: Flames from a Vietcong rocket attack light night sky over the U.S. base at Danang.

troops and Vietcong were in position.

The night before Tet began, North Vietnamese radio broadcast a poem:

Let North and South emulate each other in fighting the U.S aggressors! Forward! Total victory will be ours.

The author was Ho Chi Minh.

The first attacks of the Tet Offensive began just after midnight on January 30, a day before the major attacks were scheduled. Six cities and several American and ARVN airfields and bases came under mortar and rocket fire. The attacks alarmed some American commanders. They were especially puzzled by a rocket attack on the city of Pleiku. The Vietcong had attacked Pleiku several times, but they had concentrated on military targets around the city. This time the focus of the attack was the city itself. South Vietnamese officers, however, believed the January 30 attacks were just isolated incidents. The Vietcong were not strong enough to attack the cities of South Vietnam, they said.

Early on the morning of the 31st the offensive began in earnest. Fighting broke out in almost every corner of South Vietnam, even in towns and cities that had been considered secure for years. Vietcong guerrillas, under cover of darkness and mortar fire, attacked their assigned targets with grim determination. Often the guerrillas were followed by NVA troops. "The surprise," one South Vietnamese officer said later, "was total."

Most surprising was the fighting in and around Saigon. Saigon, with its population of two million people, was considered an island of security. For years it had been spared the fighting that had destroyed much of the country. That changed at 1:30 A.M. on January 31, 1968. Four thousand Vietcong guerrillas had made their way into Saigon. Dividing into small teams, they fanned out through the streets to their targets. They penetrated the heavily fortified U.S. embassy, fired rockets into the grounds of the Presidential Palace, and stormed ARVN general headquarters. Saigon's airport, Tan Son Nhut, was attacked and nearly overrun. The sky above the city was lit by flames from burning munitions dumps. The Vietcong seemed to be everywhere. General Frederick Weyand, monitoring the attacks on an electronic map, said later that the map lit up "like a pinball machine."

One of the major Vietcong targets was the South Vietnamese government radio station. An elite Vietcong unit had trained for three months to capture it. They drove a dynamite-packed car into the building's gate and blasted their way in. Just as they were about to announce the "liberation" of Saigon over the air, the South Vietnamese managed to shut the transmitter down. The guerrillas barricaded themselves in the building, waiting for a relief force. It never arrived. When morning came, South Vietnamese troops stormed the radio station. Dang Xuan Teo, one of the few Vietcong survivors of the attack, later described what happened: "We were down to eight men. . . . The comrades decided I should try to get away, report to our superiors, and return with orders. I managed to escape. Soon afterward, though, they detonated the explosives, blowing up the building and sacrificing themselves."

Despite the surprise attacks, the Americans and the ARVN recovered quickly. They began to take back the streets from the Vietcong. Helicopter gunships and jets arrived to help the infantry. Over the next few days the Vietcong were driven from their hiding places in the city and its suburbs. They failed to hold a single one of their objectives. But the Battle of Saigon had taken a terrible toll. Much of the city lay in ruins. Thousands of people had been made homeless—many of them refugees from the countryside who had already suffered the destruction of their villages.

On February 1, General Westmoreland reported that the offensive was "about to run out of steam." The next day, President Johnson, eager to reassure a shocked American public, called the offensive "a complete failure" but added that "the situation is still fluid." It was to remain fluid for almost a month. In most of the country, U.S. and South Vietnamese forces regained control quickly. But the Vietcong and NVA had managed to gain footholds in some towns and cities. The worst fighting took place in the coastal city of Hue.

Many people considered Hue, once the seat of Vietnam's emperors, the most beautiful city in Vietnam. Hue's centerpiece was the Citadel, a city-

U.S. ARMY PHOTO

An American soldier moves cautiously through a Saigon street the day after the first furious Tet attacks.

within-a-city of temples and palaces. To the Vietnamese people, Hue was a symbol of Vietnam's golden age. The North Vietnamese knew that to capture Hue would be a powerful psychological victory.

At 3:40 A.M. on the morning of January 31, mortar shells and rockets crashed into Hue. Shortly afterward several regiments of NVA troops swept through the city's ARVN defenders. When the first U.S. Marine reinforcements arrived the next day, they were greeted by a red-starred Vietcong flag

U.S. MARINE CORPS PHOTO

A marine dashes for cover as a Vietcong sniper opens fire in Hue.

flying above the Citadel. The NVA and Vietcong had occupied much of the city. It took 25 days of bitter house-to-house fighting for American and South Vietnamese troops to retake Hue.

A U.S. marine officer compared the fighting in Hue with city combat in the Korean War: "Seoul was tough . . . but this—well, it's something else." Casualties were heavy. In the fighting to retake the Citadel, one battalion lost a marine killed or wounded for every yard of territory gained. An American reporter later wrote, "On the worst days, no one expected to get through it alive."

When Hue was finally secured, mass graves were discovered on the outskirts of the city. They contained the remains of civilians executed by the Vietcong. While their fighting comrades were battling American and ARVN troops, Vietcong political cadres had set up a "revolutionary government" in the occupied areas of Hue. This government had executed citizens of Hue who had supported the South Vietnamese government or the Americans. They also killed students, civil servants, priests, and policemen—anyone considered an "enemy of the revolution." One woman described what happened to her father: "The Communists came to our house and questioned my father, who was an elderly official about to retire. Then they went away. . . . My mother and I were worried because the Communists had arrested his father in just that way in 1946. Like his father, my father never came back." The exact number of people executed in Hue is not known. Estimates run from 3,000 to nearly 6,000.

The situation was similar throughout the rest of South Vietnam. In most places, the worst of the battle was borne by civilians. Some 14,000 died in the offensive. Half a million became refugees. Many villages and towns were damaged or even destroyed in the fighting. One such community was Ben Tre, in the Mekong Delta. The Vietcong had gained a particularly strong foothold in Ben Tre, and half the town was flattened by American bombs and shells before they were driven out. An American officer told a journalist, "It became necessary to destroy the town in order to save it."

By the beginning of March the Tet Offensive was over. The NVA and Vietcong had been driven from the cities. Khe Sanh had not fallen, although it would be another month before an American relief force broke through the jungle and lifted the 77-day siege.

General Westmoreland proclaimed Tet a victory for the United States and for South Vietnam. Tet was indeed a smashing defeat for the NVA and Vietcong. Despite their careful planning and furious attacks, they had gained no territory. The general uprising they had placed so much faith in did not happen. They had been surprised by the stiff resistance put up by some South Vietnamese units. The Vietcong and the NVA had little regard for the ARVN's ability to fight in the countryside, but with their homes and families threatened, many South Vietnamese soldiers fought with skill and determination.

The Communist forces had suffered great losses. As many as 50,000 NVA and Vietcong may have died in the offensive, 10,000 at Khe Sanh alone, against 2,600 American and South Vietnamese troops killed and some 12,000 wounded. Ho and Giap's gamble had failed. After the war, Duong Quynh Hoa, who had fought with the Vietcong in Saigon, called Tet "a grievous miscalculation" on Hanoi's part. Another former Vietcong guerrilla said simply, "We lost our best people."

But battles are not lost or won on the battlefield alone. The Tet Offensive led the United States to question its involvement in Vietnam more than any other event in the war. Before Tet, the American public had been led to believe that war was not only winnable but being won. And yet the enemy had been able to launch an offensive along the length and breadth of South Vietnam. The reaction of a journalist to the attack on the U.S. embassy in Saigon—"I thought we were winning this war!"—summed up the confusion felt by many Americans. After Tet, cries for an end to the conflict swelled to a roar.

The military victory won by the United States and South Vietnam turned into a psychological victory for the Communists. The first sign of this came when General Westmoreland, aware of how badly the enemy had been beaten, asked for 206,000 more troops to crush the NVA and the Vietcong completely, in addition to the 525,000 American troops already in South Vietnam. Westmoreland wanted the troops right away—by May 1. Such an action would have meant calling up large numbers of reserves, and that would have been extremely unpopular, especially in an election year. Many in Washington urged President Johnson to grant his request. Johnson refused. On March 13 he agreed only to send 10,300 replacements and 30,000 reservists to Vietnam, a far lower number than Westmoreland wanted. Johnson realized that the majority of Americans would not support a widening of the war after the shock of Tet.

Even conservative newspapers began to question the war. An editorial in the *Wall Street Journal* in February 1968 cautioned, "The American people should be getting ready to accept, if they haven't already, the prospect that the whole Vietnam effort may be doomed." The newspaper headlines and the images flashing across TV screens had caused a great shift in American public opinion. Walter Cronkite, perhaps the most famous and trusted American television reporter, had been in Vietnam during most of Tet. On February 27, back in the United States, he told millions of viewers that "[it is] more certain than ever that the bloody experience of Vietnam is to end in a stalemate." His report convinced many ordinary Americans to question the wisdom of remaining in Vietnam.

Tran Do, a North Vietnamese officer and one of the planners of the offensive, described Tet's impact: "In all honesty, we didn't achieve our main objective, which was to spur uprisings throughout the South. Still, we inflicted heavy casualties on the Americans and their puppets. As for making an impact in the United States, it had not been our intention—but it was a fortunate result."

President Johnson was facing political problems at home. On March 12, the New Hampshire presidential primary was held. Senator Eugene McCarthy, a critic of the war, won 42 percent of the vote against Johnson's 48 percent—a very slim lead for an incumbent president. Four days later, Senator Robert F. Kennedy, brother of the slain president

With his popularity dropping after the shock of Tet, President Johnson tells the nation he will not seek reelection on March 31, 1968.

THE LYNDON B. JOHNSON LIBRARY

and now a critic of the war, announced his candidacy.

On March 31, President Johnson went on national television. Looking tired and drawn, he said, "Tonight I want to speak to you on peace in Vietnam and Southeast Asia." He announced an almost complete halt in the bombing of North Vietnam, and called upon President Ho Chi Minh "to respond positively and favorably to this new step toward peace." He noted that 1968 was an election year and that he was expected to run for reelection. But, said Johnson,

> With America's sons in the field far away . . . and the world's hopes for peace in the balance every day, I do not believe I should devote an hour or a day of my time to any duties other than . . . the presidency of your country. Accordingly, I shall not seek and I will not accept the nomination of my party for another term as your president.

Johnson's withdrawal from the presidential race was a surprise to even his closest advisers, and it shocked many Americans. Reporters had nicknamed him "the political animal" for his love of campaigning. Many of the ambitious Great Society programs he had begun four years before remained unfinished. But the war had taken its toll on Johnson. A recent poll had found that only 36 percent of Americans approved of his presidency. In the wake of the Tet Offensive, another poll revealed that only 26 percent approved of his handling of the war. The growing opposition to the war in the streets and on the college campuses of the United States, as well as in his own cabinet, troubled Johnson greatly. He had decided to forgo the presidential race to try to seek peace. Lyndon Johnson's presidency had become another casualty of the war in Vietnam.

Three days after Johnson's surprise announcement, the government of North Vietnam agreed to participate in negotiations. On April 7, U.S. bombing was halted north of the 19th parallel in North Vietnam. On May 13, delegates from North Vietnam and the United States met in Paris and began talks aimed at ending the conflict. It seemed as if peace might be near. But more than four more years of war would pass before the last American combat troops left Vietnam.

THE LIVING ROOM WAR

Because the news media brought the war into almost every American household, Vietnam has been called the Living Room War. Many outstanding journalists covered the conflict, including reporters David Halberstam of the *New York Times*, Michael Herr of *Esquire* magazine, Malcolm Browne of the Associated Press, and Neil Sheehan of United Press International; photographers Tim Page and Eddie Adams; and TV reporter Walter Cronkite. Public reaction to the images they sent from Vietnam—images of dead and injured civilians, burning villages, and towns reduced to ruins—led many to question American involvement and helped bring the war to an end.

Some people have criticized the news media's influence on the war. They believe the media often portrayed the American effort poorly, paying more attention to sensational stories like the My Lai massacre than to military victories and "nation-building" programs in South Vietnam. Critics believe the media lowered the morale of American troops and encouraged the enemy.

This conflict between freedom of the press and military necessity has continued into the 1980s. Reporters were not allowed on the island of Grenada during the American invasion in October 1983, and Britain censored news reports during its 1982 war with Argentina in the Falkland Islands. The question of whether a democratic society can have complete freedom of the press in time of war still remains to be answered.

The photographs on these pages, most of them sad or shocking, are among of the best-remembered images of the Vietnam War.

WIDE WORLD PHOTOS

On June 11, 1963, Quang Ngai, a Buddhist monk, set himself on fire as a protest against the policies of South Vietnamese President Ngo Dinh Diem. Several others followed his example.

WIDE WORLD PHOTOS

General Nguyen Ngoc Loan, Chief of South Vietnam's National Police, executes a Vietcong guerrilla on a Saigon street on February 1, 1968. This photograph, taken during the height of the fighting in Saigon during Tet, was the work of veteran photographer Eddie Adams.

©1969 LIFE PICTURE SERVICE

This photograph shows some of the 300 civilians shot by American troops in the village of My Lai in March 1968. When the incident was revealed in 1969, a shock wave of outrage spread through the United States.

WIDE WORLD PHOTOS

A terrified Vietnamese girl flees down a road after an accidental South Vietnamese napalm strike burned off her clothes. This shocking and tragic picture captures the suffering the war brought to Vietnam's civilians.

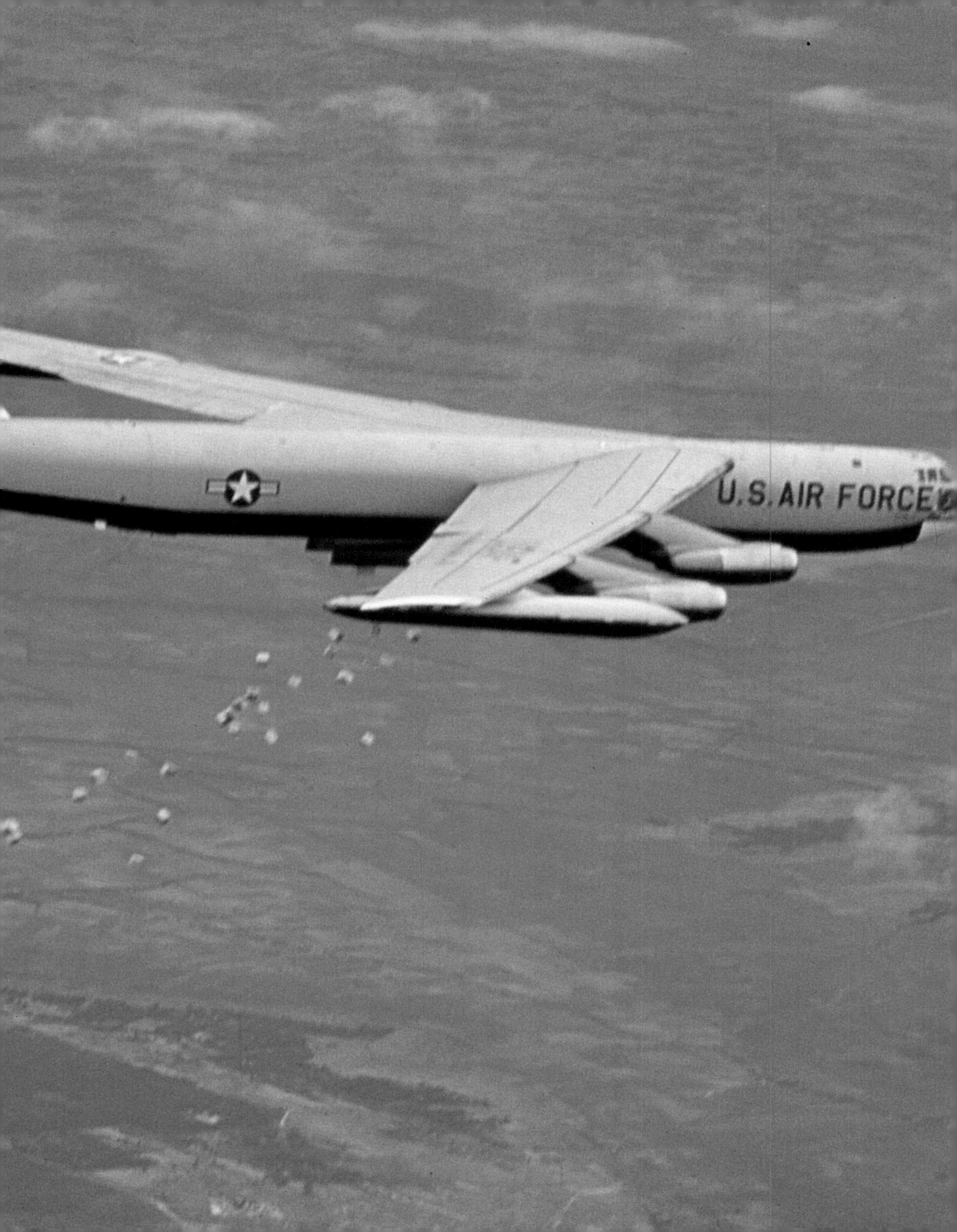
U.S. AIR FORCE

4

"VIETNAMIZATION" AND DEFEAT

The presidential election of 1968 was one of the stormiest in American history. The most important issue for both major parties was the war in Vietnam.

On April 27, 1968, Vice President Hubert Humphrey announced his candidacy. Senator Robert F. Kennedy, a leading contender for the Democratic nomination, was assassinated in Los Angeles in June. Many young people rallied behind Senator Eugene McCarthy, the most antiwar of the candidates. In a campaign speech, McCarthy used Tet to support his views:

> In 1963, we were told that we were winning the war . . . and now again in 1968, we hear the same hollow claims of programs and victory. Only a few months ago we were told that 65 percent of the population was secure. Now we know that not even the American embassy is secure.

An Air Force B-52 bombs a Vietcong position.

Despite his popularity with young people, McCarthy lacked a broad base of support. When the Democratic Convention opened in Chicago in that summer, it seemed likely that Hubert Humphrey, a moderate on the war, would receive the nomination.

The Chicago convention was marked by bitter debate on the convention floor and violence on the streets outside. Some antiwar Democrats demanded a resolution calling for an immediate end to all bombing of North Vietnam and the withdrawal of all American troops. Moderates, led by Humphrey, favored peace talks but wanted to withdraw American forces only if North Vietnam also removed its troops from South Vietnam. Humphrey's resolution won, but it split the party.

Crowds of protestors, many of them students, had gathered in Chicago to protest against the war. Bloody riots between police and demonstrators broke

U.S. AIR FORCE PHOTO

62 9,000
63 15,000
64 23,000
65 184,000
66 268,000
67 449,000
68 535,000
69 542,000
70 415,000
71 239,000
72 47,000

SIMON HU

American troop strength in Vietnam, 1962–1972.

out on August 28. The evening news ran footage of helmeted riot police wading into crowds of demonstrators, clubbing and beating many of them.

Meanwhile, a third party, the American Independent Party, had joined the race. The party's leader and presidential nominee, former Alabama governor George C. Wallace, stressed "law and order." He wanted victory in Vietnam, by negotiation if possible but by force if necessary. His running mate was former Air Force General Curtis LeMay. LeMay was a hard-line hawk who had once said it would be possible for the United States to "bomb the North Vietnamese back into the stone age."

The Republicans chose Richard Nixon, formerly vice president under Eisenhower, as their candidate. Nixon, too, pledged to seek a negotiated peace in Vietnam. On October 31, 1968, just days before the election, President Johnson announced an end to all air, naval, and artillery bombardment of North Vietnam. The move gained some support for Humphrey, Johnson's chosen successor. But public opinion had swung to the Republicans, especially after the violence at the Democratic convention. In a close race, Nixon defeated Humphrey and Wallace. He took office in January 1969, promising the American people "peace with honor."

In February 1969, the NVA and Vietcong launched another offensive in South Vietnam. While much smaller than Tet a year before, the attacks caused heavy American casualties. President Nixon ordered a bombing campaign against communist sanctuaries in Cambodia.

The bombings, called Operation Menu, went on for fourteen months. They were conducted in secret without the knowledge or approval of Congress. In May 1969, the *New York Times* reported the bombings. At the time, Operation Menu caused little public outcry, but during the Watergate Scandal, which unfolded in the early 1970s, these illegal bombings became a major issue.

While the United States chose a president, the Paris Peace Talks had become bogged down over petty details. In May 1969, Nixon proposed a peace plan based on free, supervised elections in South Vietnam and the withdrawal of both American and North Vietnamese troops. But the North Vietnamese demanded removal of the "puppet regime" in Saigon before any agreement could be reached.

In June, after a conference with South Vietnamese President Nguyen Van Thieu on Midway Island in the South Pacific, Nixon announced that 110,000 American troops would be withdrawn before the end of 1969. He also appealed to Ho Chi Minh for help in breaking the deadlocked talks. His appeal was rejected. But while the talks appeared to be accomplishing nothing, Nixon's National Security Adviser, Henry Kissinger, was meeting secretly with representatives of the North Vietnamese government to negotiate an end to the war.

President Nixon announced a program of "Vietnamization." Vietnamization was a plan for a gradual troop withdrawal. American forces would concentrate on training the ARVN to deal with the enemy on its own.

In the summer and fall of 1969, protests against the war reached new heights. A national moratorium on the war was called for October 15, 1969. About 250,000 protestors gathered in Washington. Pham Van Dong, who had assumed leadership of North Vietnam after Ho Chi Minh's death in September, sent greetings to the protesters. A second and even larger moratorium took place a month later.

But there were also Americans who took to the streets to demonstrate their support of the war—or at least their support for the men fighting it. These people felt that the South Vietnamese government, despite its problems, was still better than communism. Others argued that a withdrawal from Vietnam would encourage the spread of communism in other parts of the world. Many Americans were angered at the sight of young people protesting the war while other young Americans were fighting and dying. A mother whose son was in Vietnam said she could not

U.S. ARMY PHOTO

An American "tunnel rat," a soldier trained to fight the Vietcong in their underground hide-outs, emerges from a tunnel near Chu Lai in 1969.

understand "how they [antiwar demonstrators] get off while my son has to go over there and maybe get his head shot off." But as the war dragged on and casualties mounted, people from all parts of American society joined the protests.

On November 16, 1969, the Pentagon revealed an incident that had taken place in the wake of the Tet Offensive over a year before.

On March 16, 1968, a U.S. army company had swept into the village of My Lai–4 in Quang Ngai province. The company had been patrolling the area for weeks. It had suffered heavy casualties, mostly from snipers and booby traps. Their captain told them they would have the chance to "get even" with the Vietcong.

The soldiers found no Vietcong. In their frustration, they turned their guns against the village's civilians. Between 300 and 400 people were killed before an American officer landed and stopped the madness.

The news shocked even supporters of the war and fanned the flames of protest. In November 1970, Lieutenant William Calley, an officer accused of participating in the massacre, was tried for the murder of South Vietnamese civilians. He was found guilty and sentenced to life imprisonment, but within several years his sentence was reduced, and he was eventually paroled—which further angered many Americans.

After Tet, there was growing unrest among the troops in Vietnam as the division sweeping the United States affected the American forces. Soldiers were angered by news stories showing demonstrators waving Vietcong flags. They felt that their service and sacrifices were not understood or appreciated. They resented antiwar protesters who avoided the draft and who called American soldiers "baby killers." The strain of fighting an often invisible enemy among a civilian population that could be openly resentful took its toll on morale. In some units, discipline broke down. Drug abuse became a problem. Sometimes, unpopular officers were killed by their own men. Some troops simply refused to go into the field.

In the spring of 1970, the war spilled over from Vietnam into the neighboring nation of Cambodia. Cambodia was supposedly neutral, but the jungle along its border with South Vietnam provided sanctuaries for NVA troops and supplies. In April 1970, President Nixon gave American commanders permission to cross the border, and on April 29, American and South Vietnamese troops invaded sections of Cambodia. The two-month operation was a short-term military success. Large quantities of supplies and weapons were captured. The American casualty rate in South Vietnam dropped.

But the invasion touched off a fresh round of antiwar protests in the United States. On May 4, National Guardsmen fired into a crowd of demonstrators at Kent State University in Ohio, killing four students. Violence swept the nation's campuses. Within a week, 448 colleges had temporarily shut down.

American troops continued to be withdrawn from Vietnam. By the end of 1970, American troop strength had dropped to 415,000, from a 1969 high of 542,000. The next year it would fall to 239,000, the lowest level since 1966.

Early in 1971, Vietnamization was put to the test when South Vietnamese troops pushed into Laos to try to destroy the NVA supply route along the

A student cries over the body of an antiwar protestor, one of four killed during a confrontation between students and national guardsmen at Kent State University in Ohio on May 4, 1970.

© VALLEY NEWS SERVICE

Ho Chi Minh trail. American troops were not permitted to cross the border into Laos, but the ARVN received American air and artillery support.

The operation was a failure. The South Vietnamese fought badly, and the NVA drove them back across the border. The situation worsened in March 1972, when twelve NVA divisions openly invaded South Vietnam across the DMZ. Only American air support and a determined stand by the best South Vietnamese troops held the NVA back.

President Nixon ordered a massive bombing campaign against North Vietnam in retaliation, the first such campaign since 1968. He also ordered all North Vietnamese ports mined and blockaded, including the chief port, Haiphong Harbor. These actions led to another wave of antiwar protests in the United States, but they also broke the deadlock that had gripped the Paris Peace Talks. Despite the air attacks on North Vietnam, U.S. troops continued to be withdrawn. On August 13, 1972, the last American combat troops left South Vietnam. All that remained was a handful of support troops and airmen. On October 23, 1972, Nixon ordered that the bombing of North Vietnam be stopped north of the 20th parallel. On October 26, Henry Kissinger an-

On January 23, 1973, Henry Kissinger and Le Duc Tho sign the long-awaited peace agreement in Paris. The agreement took the United States out of the war but did not bring peace to Vietnam.

INDOCHINA ARCHIVES, BERKELEY

A group of American prisoners of war prepares to leave Hanoi after the signing of the Paris peace agreement in January 1973. The North Vietnamese treatment of American POWs was brutal.

U.S. NAVY PHOTO

nounced, "Peace is at hand." Partly on the strength of Kissinger's statement, Nixon was reelected a few days later.

The announcement was premature. The negotiations again fell apart, and on December 18 Nixon ordered the bombing of North Vietnam north of the 20th parallel resumed. The saturation bombings of Hanoi and Haiphong were the heaviest of the war. These so-called Christmas bombings caused worldwide protest. Finally, on January 23, 1973, a cease-fire agreement was reached between Kissinger and Le Duc Tho, the chief North Vietnamese negotiator. There were 145,000 North Vietnamese troops in South Vietnam, and under the terms of the agreement they were al-

lowed to remain. An international commission was appointed to oversee a cease-fire. American prisoners of war were released from North Vietnam.

Four days later the cease-fire began. America's longest war had ended. Almost 60,000 Americans had died. The Vietnam War had divided the United States as had no other conflict since the Civil War.

But the departure of the Americans did not bring peace to Indochina. South Vietnam had come to depend on the United States to prop up its economy, its government, and its military. With American aid reduced, South Vietnam's economy nearly collapsed. The Saigon government, led by President Nguyen

Van Thieu, remained unstable. Few people believed that the South Vietnamese armed forces could cope with the North Vietnamese threat now that American air support and firepower had gone. In parts of the country, fighting continued despite the cease-fire. Some villages openly flew the Vietcong flag. President Thieu, who had signed the cease-fire only at American insistence, was gloomy about South Vietnam's chances for survival.

The "peace that never was," as one writer called it, lasted less than three years. On December 6, 1974, NVA troops, well supplied with tanks and artillery, invaded and captured the entire South Vietnamese province of Phuoc Long. Then, in February 1975, Hanoi launched a full-scale invasion of South Vietnam. Some 200,000 NVA troops moved steadily south, driving huge columns of refugees before them. The ARVN fell back, hoping to hold Saigon and the populated areas around it, but this strategy failed before the NVA's relentless advance.

By April, the North Vietnamese were 40 miles from Saigon. President Ford made a last-ditch appeal to Congress for $772 million in emergency military aid to South Vietnam. It was refused. Four days later Thieu fled to Taiwan. He blamed the United States for not sending money or troops to help South Vietnam, calling the lack of support "an inhumane act by an inhumane ally."

South Vietnamese refugees flee as the North Vietnamese advance toward Saigon in the spring of 1975.

U.S. ARMY PHOTO

UPI/BETTMANN NEWSPHOTOS

April 29, 1975—With North Vietnamese tanks on the outskirts of the city, a line of American civilians and their Vietnamese employees and dependents climb to the rooftop helipad of the American embassy in Saigon.

On April 27, NVA rockets began to hit Saigon. Washington ordered Operation Frequent Wind, the evacuation of the last American diplomatic and military personnel and as many of their Vietnamese dependents and employees as possible. U.S. Navy ships took up station off the coast to receive the thousands of Vietnamese fleeing aboard boats and aircraft. On April 29, Graham Martin, the last U.S. ambassador to South Vietnam, left Saigon. The next morning, the embassy's marine guards boarded the last helicopter and flew to the waiting ships as North Vietnamese tanks and infantry advanced through the streets of Saigon. Three decades of war had ended in a shattering defeat for South Vietnam and its chief ally, the United States.

The cost in death and suffering was terribly high. Over 220,000 South Vietnamese military personnel had been killed. The NVA and Vietcong lost an estimated 444,000 people. The worst suffering was endured by the civilians of South Vietnam and its neighboring nations: about 587,000 had been killed and 9 million made homeless.

North and South Vietnam were soon united under Communist leadership. This government has brought unity to Vietnam but not peace or prosperity. Despite a pledge of amnesty, some 400,000 members of the former South Vietnamese government and military were sent to reeducation camps after the Communist victory. Vietnamese of Chinese ancestry suffered especially severely, since Vietnam had broken ranks with its former ally, Communist China. As many as 500,000 refugees have fled Vietnam, either overland or in unseaworthy boats. Thousands of these "boat people" died at sea in their attempt to reach freedom. Many Vietnamese refugees have settled in the United States.

Today, Vietnam's economy is weak, and corruption and inefficiency are now problems for the Communist government. Pham Van Dong, Vietnam's leader, told an American journalist in 1981, "Yes, we defeated the United States. But now we are plagued by problems. We do not have enough to eat. We are a poor, undeveloped nation. You know, waging a war is very simple, but running a country is very difficult."

Continuing warfare in Southeast Asia has added to this difficulty. Just before Saigon fell, the communist Khmer Rouge guerrillas took control of Cambodia. For the next four years their fanatical regime conducted a reign of terror that left between two and four million Cambodians dead. In December 1978, Vietnam invaded Cambodia, finally putting an end to the Khmer Rouge terror. But in the process Vietnam angered Communist China, who supported the Khmer Rouge. In February 1979, the Chinese launched a 17-day invasion of Vietnam in retaliation.

Vietnam is now an ally of the Soviet Union—one of the reasons for the hostility between Vietnam and China. Soviet ships and planes now occupy bases built by the United States. Soviet influence in Vietnam has led to a shift in the balance of political and military power in the whole Pacific region.

The hard lesson learned in Vietnam was a turning point in American foreign policy. In November 1973, Congress passed the War Powers Act over President Nixon's veto. Congress realized the dangers of giving the president a "blank check" to wage war, as it had done nine years earlier with the Gulf of Tonkin Resolution. The War Powers Act made it illegal for the president to commit U.S. forces to combat overseas for more than 60 days without the approval of Congress.

The war created a "Vietnam syndrome" in America's international affairs. Since Vietnam, the United States has been cautious about sending its troops overseas. The fear of "another Vietnam" has prevented the United States from intervening in trouble spots like Central America as forcefully as it had in Southeast Asia years before.

The Vietnam War was an economic turning point for the United States, too. From 1965 to 1973, the Vietnam War cost the United States some $150 billion. President Lyndon Johnson had been reluctant to raise taxes for the war effort, so the government borrowed heavily. This was a politically successful strategy in the short run. In fact, the years from 1961 to 1969 saw the longest period of sustained economic growth in the nation's history. But in the mid–1970s, the economic effects of the war were felt. The growing national debt, combined with inflation, higher energy costs, and unemployment, led to a condition economists call "stagflation." Stagflation means a sluggish economy with high inflation and little growth. Inflation and unemployment declined in the 1980s, but the enormous national debt remains. This debt has been made worse by the major American military buildup in the 1980s—which again was paid for mostly by borrowing, not by taxes. As a result, the United States is now the world's largest debtor nation.

It is almost impossible to sum up the meaning of the Vietnam War in a few words. The war that raged in that small Asian nation for nearly a decade touched the lives of every American in one way or another. The war's impact is still felt in many areas of our society. For this reason, we must learn about Vietnam and try to understand it. The hardest lessons are often the most valuable.

AFTERWORD

THE MEMORIAL

In earlier American wars, most soldiers returned home with their units. In Vietnam, men entered and left the war zone as individuals. After their tour of duty—usually a year or thirteen months—they boarded chartered jet planes and were flown back to what they called "the World." Often it was a lonely homecoming.

Vietnam was a humiliating experience for the United States. After the last troops came home, and after Saigon fell, the country tried to forget Vietnam. But in the process, they forgot the men and women who had served and suffered there. Many Vietnam veterans felt betrayed by their country. They had answered when their country had called, and yet their country seemed to ignore them when they returned.

Many could not find jobs. The veterans' benefits they received were less than those given to veterans of World War II or the Korean War. Many vets were angry that draft evaders received a

A few of the more than 57,000 names on the wall.

presidential pardon. Some began to suffer a variety of illnesses because of their exposure to Agent Orange, a chemical compound widely used to destroy plant cover in Vietnam. Thousands of veterans were physically disabled for life, and thousands more were wounded emotionally. Many vets suffered recurring nightmares about combat and the death and suffering they had seen in Vietnam. While the majority of vets came home and resumed normal, productive lives, some vets, haunted by their experiences, dropped out of society.

Philip Caputo served with the U.S. Marines in 1965. His book, *A Rumor of War*, was one of the first to describe the war from the point of view of the ordinary infantryman. The passage below describes his reaction to a close friend's death in combat:

You were faithful. Your country is not. As I write this, the country for which you died wishes to forget the war in which you died. Its very name is a curse. There are no monuments to its heroes, no statues in small-town squares and city parks, no plaques and wreaths and memorials. For plaques and wreaths and memorials are reminders, and they would make it harder for your country to sink into the amnesia for which it longs. It wishes to forget and it has forgotten.

In March 1979, a former army infantryman, Jan Scruggs, went to see a movie about Vietnam. That night, Scruggs was haunted by memories of the men he had served with who never returned home. Scruggs realized that what he and other vets wanted most was the recognition that they had suffered and sacrificed for their country. He decided to work toward building a Vietnam War memorial—a memorial not to the war itself but to the individual men and women who had given their lives. With several other vets, he formed the Vietnam Veterans Memorial Fund. Slowly, money came in, mostly in small amounts, from veterans or the families of those that died. But as word of the VVMF's efforts spread, more donations began to come in from all over the country.

Next, the VVMF appealed to a congressional committee for land in Washington, D.C., for the memorial site. Robert Doubek, the VVMF's legal counselor and a vet himself, addressed the committee:

> Over 2.7 million Americans served in Vietnam. More than 57,000 died and over 300,000 were wounded. . . . The Vietnam Veterans Memorial is conceived as a means to promote the healing and reconciliation of the country after the divisions caused by the war.

It will symbolize the experience of the Vietnam generation for the generations that will follow.

On April 30, 1980, a bill was passed authorizing a two-acre site in the heart of the capital, near the Washington, Jefferson, and Lincoln memorials.

The VVMF then held a nationwide competition to find a design for the memorial, and 1,421 designs were submitted. The winning design was the work of a 21-year-old architecture student, Maya Ying Lin. Her concept was simple and striking: two long walls of polished black granite, sloping into the ground. On the panels would be engraved the names of all the American servicemen and -women killed in Vietnam, in the chronological order of their deaths.

The design touched off a storm of controversy. Critics found fault with the color of the granite, the downward angle of the walls—and the whole concept behind the design. Some called it "a mere tombstone," a "black gash of shame." To satisfy those who wanted a more conventional memorial, the VVMF approved plans for a simple, dignified sculpture of three weary infantrymen to be built on the memorial grounds near the wall. But the VVMF insisted Maya Lin's design be used for the main part of the monument. On March 26, 1982, ground was broken.

In November 1982, a four-day National Salute to Vietnam Veterans was held in Washington, D.C., and 150,000 vets poured into Washington from every corner of the country for a long-delayed homecoming. On Saturday, November 15, 15,000 veterans marched

NATIONAL PARK SERVICE

Vietnam veterans from all over the nation gathered in Washington for the memorial's dedication on November 13, 1982.

down Constitution Avenue past cheering crowds. The Vietnam vets had come home at last. That afternoon, the three-year effort to build a memorial to those who never returned ended as the Vietnam Veterans Memorial was officially dedicated. In late 1988, plans were announced for an addition to the memorial commemorating women who had served in Vietnam.

Millions of people have visited the memorial since 1982. Veterans come to remember their fallen friends. The families of those who died search for the name of a brother, a husband, or a father on the smooth black walls. As they reach up to touch it, they see their own reflections in the polished stone. Many leave things at the memorial in silent tribute: a flower, a poem, a flag, a photograph. The Vietnam Veterans Memorial has achieved its purpose. More than anything else, it has helped heal the rift that the Vietnam War left on the soul of America.

NATIONAL PARK SERVICE

The statue at the entrance plaza to the Vietnam Veterans Memorial in Washington, DC.

INDEX

SUGGESTED READING

BECKETT, IAN. *Vietnam From 1945*. New York: Gallery Books, 1986.

The Illustrated History of the Vietnam War (series). New York: Bantam Books, 1987.

KARNOW, STANLEY. *Vietnam: A History*. New York: Penguin, 1984.

The Vietnam Experience (series). Boston: Boston Publishing Company, 1981.